The Divine Wisdom of Prophet Muhammad

Debates of Prophet Muhammad

with scholars and representatives of five religions

Translated by

Fiza Reza

Edited and Annotated by

Abu Yahya al-Hosseini

Author: Abu Ali Fadhl ibn Hasan Tabresi
Translator: Fiza Reza
Editor and Annotator: Abu Yahya al-Hosseini
Graphics: M. Khalil
Publisher: Jerrmein Abu Shahba
ISBN: 978-1-7330284-1-7
Year: 2019

Copyright Notice

This book is protected by copyright. Publication in any form is prohibited and requires prior permission from Publisher

Contents

Preface I

Translator's Note v

Chapter 1 1

Part 1: Debate with Jews 3

Part 2: Debate with Christians 7

Part 3: Debate with Atheists 13

Part 4: Debate with Dualists [*Sanaviyas*] 17

Part 5: Debate with Polytheists 19

Chapter 2 25

Chapter 3 43

Glossary of key terms 49

Index 53

Debates of Prophet Muhammad (pbuh)

Preface

The present book entitled "The Divine Wisdom of the Holy Prophet Muhammad [pbuh], Debates of Holy Prophet Muhammad [pbuh] with scholars and representatives of other religions", translated from *Ihtajaj al-Tabarsi* by Fizza Haidari, edited and annotated by Abu Yahya al-Hosseini is being published by the Islamic Research Foundation of the Holy Shrine of Imam Reza (as), Mashhad, Islamic Republic of Iran.

This work includes debates of the Holy Prophet Muhammad [pbuh] with scholars and representatives of the Judaism, Christianity, atheism, dualism and polytheism in three chapters and the chapter one is divided into five parts. The glossary of key terms is also provided for the readers of this book.

Publication of the present work can be considered as the dire need of the time because ceaseless false, baseless and vicious propaganda is being carried out against the Holy Prophet Muhammad [pbuh] by the Zionist controlled Western mass media to create Islamophobia in the world. But the debates of the Holy Prophet Muhammad [pbuh] with scholars and representatives of other religions prove that the dynamic universal message of Islam was preached through peace and brotherhood.

As the Almighty Allah's Final, Last and Greatest Messenger, entrusted with the universal message of Islam, the Holy Prophet Muhammad [pbuh] preached Islam by dialogue, reasoning and rational approach. These were the factors that led to the rapid spread of the message of *Tawhid* (monotheism) and virtue in his lifetime in the Arabian Peninsula and beyond. In accordance with the commandments of God revealed through the *ayahs* of the Holy Qur'an, the Final and Last Testament from Almighty Allah, he invited the Arab polytheists, Jews and Christians, as well as the Zoroastrians to contemplate on the rationality of Islam and acknowledge it as the final and universal creed of mankind. The Holy Prophet's politeness had a great impact on all those who came into contact with him. He used to say I have been raised to complete the best morals. His courteous behavior and his modesty, in addition to his already famous reputation as *Sadeq* (Truthful) and *Amin* (Trustworthy) had an electrifying impact on the people of Makkah and Medina, in molding their life as per the directives of the Holy Qur'an.

Despite persecution by the oligarch rich pagans in Makkah that saw its vested interests in exploiting fellow human beings in danger, the message of Islam spread, through the patience, endurance, and rational teachings of Holy Prophet Muhammad [pbuh], who invited people to ponder. In the face of divine logic and reasoning, the pressures, tortures and even killing of early Muslims by the pagan Arabs were useless. Even the three year economic and social boycott imposed by the pagan Arabs on the Holy Prophet [pbuh] and the new Muslim community was useless, thanks to the devotion and loyalty of the Holy Prophet's uncle and guardian, Abu Taleb (as), who took his nephew and all Muslims under his care and protection in the gorge outside Makkah, known till this day as She'b Abi Taleb.

Soon God ordered the Holy Prophet [pbuh] to migrate to Medina, and this heralded the start of a new phase in the history of Islam. Earlier several groups of people from this city, which was then called Yathreb had visited Makkah, and on being impressed by the rational teachings of the Holy Prophet [pbuh] had given their allegiance to him. They now welcomed him and through dialogue with other Arabs, as well as with the Jews and Christians, the message of Islam began to spread. Many of the pagans, the Jews, and the Christians, embraced the truth of Islam. Of those who did not, and were neither hostile, the Holy Prophet [pbuh] made pacts of neutrality with them and gave them time to contemplate and decide. Many embraced Islam and become Muslims, while the evil ones that plotted against him after sealing the agreement, he permitted them to leave Madinah by the command of God.

This is how the Holy Prophet [pbuh] won the hearts and minds. It was his routine during the season migrations of nomadic tribes to Makkah, to speak with the chieftains and others about the message that God had entrusted to his for the guidance of humanity. His equal treatment of all and his convincing discourse that all Prophets [pbut] have been sent by God in lands, but with the same universal message of monotheism and virtue, made lasting impression on the minds of all those who came into contact with him, and thus many embraced the truth of Islam.

Holy Prophet Muhammad [pbuh] was indeed the most courteous person ever. He was polite with the followers of other religions, and held dialogues with them to convince them of the truth of Islam. He did not force anybody to become Muslim, because such a conversion is useless, since real faith is from heart and with conviction. This is how Islam spread, through dialogue and discussion, and not through force, violence and the sword.

He said, if even a single person is guided towards the truth of Islam, this entails greater rewards than having red-hair camels. As the mercy to the entire creation, he never forced the Christians and Jews living under the protection of the Islamic state to change their faith, until they were convinced of the truth from the depths of their hearts. He allowed them to practice their religious rituals.

As part of his policy of peace, Holy Prophet Muhammad [pbuh] sent letters to the rulers of the then powerful empires inviting them to study Islam and come under its shade. All letters of the Holy Prophet [pbuh] started with the phrase *Bismillah-hir-Rahman-nir-Rahim*, which means 'In the Name of God, the All-Compassionate, the All-Merciful'. He used to say that reciting this dynamic phrase before embarking on any task would bring success.

The content of the Holy Prophet's letters also indicates that the Holy Prophet [pbuh] called for dialogue at the international level. In other words, enjoining good and forbidding evil was among the main messages of the Holy Prophet's epistles. The Holy Prophet's letters showed their positive effects within a short period. In this way, through dialogue and reasoning the message of Islam spread.

The Islamic Research Foundation of the Holy Shrine of Imam Reza (as) hopes that the present book titled "The Divine Wisdom of the Holy Prophet Muhammad [pbuh], Debates of Holy Prophet Muhammad [pbuh] with scholars and representatives of other religions" will pave the way for better understanding of the great divine personality of Holy Prophet Muhammad [pbuh] and the dynamic universal message of Islam.

Dr. Hyder Reza Zabeth
The Islamic Research Foundation
Astan Quds Razavi [the Holy Shrine of Imam Reza (as)]
Mashhad, Islamic Republic of Iran
2012

Translator's Note

The translation of Prophet's [pbuh] debates was inspired when we felt the need to present to the world another divine image of our beloved Prophet Mohammed [pbuh] after continuous insults to this great personality by the Western-Zionist media, the most diabolical one being the production of a movie in the early September 2012. This divine image of Prophet Muhammad [pbuh] was that of an enlightened divine scholar and an expert in extempore discussions who proved his superiority over scholars and leaders of other religions at that time.

While doing translations, effort is made to keep language as simple as possible. Footnotes are added and websites are mentioned if reader wishes to have further information. Important Arabic words are in italics. Key Arabic words explained in round brackets ( ) are described further in glossary. Difficult or less commonly used Arabic words or translated text are explained for the first time in square brackets [ ]. Prophet Muhammad's [pbuh] words are kept in double quotations " ", while all others are in single quotation marks ' '. The verses of Qur'an are in italics.

Debates of Prophet Muhammad (pbuh)

Chapter 1

Debates of Prophet Muhammad [pbuh] with scholars and representatives of five different religions

Imam Ja'far al-Sadiq [as] says that his father Imam Baqir [as] reported to him, and he was reported by Imam Ali Ibn al-Husain Zayn al-Abedin [as], who reported from his grandfather, Imam Ali [as] that once, in the city of Medina, twenty five scholars and representatives of Christianity, Judaism, Atheism, Dualism and Polytheism [five from each religion] came to see Prophet Muhammad [pbuh] and challenged him for debate... One by one they proclaimed their faith to Prophet Muhammad [pbuh]...

The Jews described their belief as: 'We believe that Prophet Uzair [Ezra] [pbuh] is a son of God and we have come to you O' Muhammad to see what you say about it. If you accept our belief then surely our religion is better than yours. And if you disagree, then we will have debate and discussion with you...'

The Christian Scholars made claim for the support of their belief as: 'We believe that God united with Messiah [Prophet Isa [pbuh], Jesus] and so Messiah is the son of God and we have come to you O' Muhammad to see what you say about it. If you accept our belief then surely our religion is better than yours. And if you disagree, then we will have debate and discussion with you...'

The Atheists made claim for the support of their belief as: 'We say that there is no time limit of this Universe, it is *qadeem*[1] (eternally pre-existent) and will remain eternal. We have come to you to see what you say about our belief. If you accept our belief then surely our religion is better than yours. And if you disagree, then in that case we will have debate and discussion with you ...'

Dualists said: 'Our belief is that Light and Darkness are the organizers of this Universe. We have come to you to see what you say about it. If you accept our belief then surely our religion is better than yours. And if you disagree then in that case we will have debate and discussion with you ...'

The polytheists of Arab made claim for the support of their belief as: 'Our belief is that our idols are our Gods. We have come to you to see what you say about our belief. If you accept our belief then surely our religion is better than yours. And if you disagree, then in that case we will have debate and discussion with you.'

When Prophet Muhammad [pbuh] heard the beliefs of all the five groups, he said: "I believe in one God Who is without any partner and I reject any other god. God has sent me as a Warner and Bearer of glad tidings for all human beings. And I am His final proof over all Universes."

---

[1] Please see glossary for more details.

Chapter 1

Part 1: Debate with Jews

Then, the Prophet [pbuh] turned towards the Jews and said: "Oh Jews! Have you come to me so that I would accept your claim without any proofs?"

The Jews replied: 'No.'

The Prophet [pbuh] said: "Then what is the reason behind your claim that Prophet Uzair [Ezra] [pbuh] is the son of God?"

The Jews replied: 'We say this because Uzair [pbuh] vivified Torah for Jews [*Bani Israel*, the nation of Prophet Musa [Moses] [pbuh]] after its destruction and he was able to do this because he was the son of God.'

The Prophet [pbuh] replied: "Now tell me why you consider Ezra [Prophet Uzair [pbuh]] as the son of God, why not Prophet Musa [pbuh] who brought Torah for Jews [*Bani Israel*] and displayed many miracles, which you are aware of. And if the only reason for you to consider Uzair [pbuh] as the son of God is his miracles of vivifying Torah then Musa [pbuh] is more worthy of being called the son of God. And if this minor miracle [vivifying of Torah] can make Uzair [pbuh] the son of God, then the one who possesses much greater miracles should have a higher status than prophethood because if by being a son you mean that man and woman copulate and give birth to a son, then you are infidels because you have compared God to His creatures and attributed to Him the characteristics of a *haadith*[2] (that which comes into

---

[2] Please see glossary for more details.

existence) and you do believe that what is *haadith* is a creature and a creature needs a Creator for its creation."

The Jews said: 'Yes, we do not think of Uzair [pbuh] as the son of God in this meaning because that would mean infidelity, just like you mentioned. But we call him the son of God to show respect towards him in the same way as some of our scholars call a person 'my son' to respect him and appreciate his high status and that person is not related to the scholar by blood because quite often, a stranger who does not have any blood relationship is also called a son. Similarly, when God did what He did to Uzair [pbuh], He made Uzair [pbuh] His son for his respect and not by birth.'

The Prophet [pbuh] said: "What you just said goes against you because if Uzair [pbuh] is the son of God because of this reason then Musa [pbuh] deserves a greater status near God. Undoubtedly, God humiliates those who deny Him instead of accepting Him and returns their argument over them. What you just said about Uzair [pbuh] being the son of God goes against you because just now, you said that a high-ranking person can call a stranger with whom he has no blood relationship his son and it is clear that he did not give birth to this person. So, you may also have seen people with high status calling a stranger their brother, or leader, or father, or master and all of these phrases are said out of respect and honour. So, the more respect a person has for another, he may call him with a higher title of praise and respect. Now that this is proven and clear to you, it will be alright for you to call Musa [pbuh] the brother of God, or His leader or father or master because it is proven that Prophet Musa [pbuh] has a greater status than Uzair [pbuh]. So, if God made Uzair [pbuh] His son out of honour, then Musa [pbuh] who possesses a higher status should be given a higher position, like His leader or uncle or lord. So will it be correct in your opinion if Musa [pbuh] is called as the brother of God or His leader or uncle or boss or master?"

Upon hearing this question from Prophet Muhammad [pbuh], all the **Jewish scholars were baffled and worried and said**: 'Oh Muhammad, give us time to think over what you said.'

The Prophet [pbuh] replied: "Yes, do think it over but think with an unbiased heart. May Allah show you the right path."

Part 2: Debate with Christians[3]

The Prophet [pbuh] then turned towards Christians and started debate…

The Prophet [pbuh] said: "You say that the *qadeem* [eternally pre-existent] God united with His son Messiah [Jesus, Prophet Isa [pbuh]]. So, in other words, you are implying that *qadeem* (God, eternally pre-existent) became *haadith* (something with a beginning) because of a *haadith* [Prophet Isa [pbuh]] and so *haadith* [Prophet Isa [pbuh]] became *qadeem*, just like God is. [means that an eternal being became contingent and the contingent became eternal].[4] Or maybe what you mean by 'God united with His son' is that God specially blessed him and did not bless anyone with the same dignity and respect. So, if by this you meant that *qadeem* God became *haadith*, then you are completely wrong. This is because it is impossible for a *qadeem* [eternally pre-existent] to become *haadith* through some revolutionary means."

"And if you say that *haadith* became *qadeem* then this is also incorrect because, just like how a *qadeem* cannot become *haadith*, a *haadith* cannot

---

[3] Prophet Muhammad [pbuh] had another debate with Christian Scholars of Najran in the year 10 A.H. On the orders of God, both parties decided to have *Mubahila* [imprecation] next day. However the Christians were frightened and backed out of *Mubahila* and agreed to pay *jizyah* [Islamic tax]. The relevant Qur'anic verses are: *But whoever disputes with you in this after what has come to you of knowledge, then say: "Come let us call our sons and your sons and our women and your women and ourselves and your selves, then let us pray earnestly and bring about the curse of Allah on the liars" (61). Most surely this is the true story, and there is no god but Allah,' and most surely Allah is the Mighty, the Wise (62). But if they turn back then surely Allah knows the mischief makers (63)* [3: 61-63]. For Qur'anic exegesis of the event of *Mubahila* from *Tafsir al-Mizan*, kindly visit: http://www.shiasource.com/al-mizan/ See under 3: 61-63.

[4] Please see glossary for more details.

become *qadeem*. And if by 'unity' you mean that God specially chose him for Himself and from among all His servants only chose Prophet Isa [pbuh] for this dignity, then this means that you have admitted on *hudooth*[5] (coming into existence) of Prophet Isa [pbuh] for which God united with him. Because when Prophet Isa [pbuh] became *haadith* [came into existence] and then God united with him, it means that he acquired 'characteristics' by which he became superior to all the creatures, then Prophet Isa [pbuh] and the new 'characteristics' are both *haadith*. And this goes against all that you have said so far."

The Christians replied: 'Oh Muhammad! When God placed great miracles [which the whole world knows] on Prophet Isa's [pbuh] hands, then He made Jesus His son to dignify and glorify him.'

The Prophet [pbuh] said: "You just heard what I said to the Jews on this topic." [And then the Prophet [pbuh] repeated his conservation with Jews]." [Please see debate of Prophet [pbuh] with Jews]

After listening to Prophet's arguments, everyone was silent. However, one person from among them came forward and said: 'Oh Muhammad! Do you not say that Abraham [Prophet Ibrahim [pbuh]] is the *Khalil* of God?'

The Prophet [pbuh] replied: "Yes, we say that."

The Christian man said: 'If Ibrahim [pbuh] can be the '*Khalil* of God', then why do you stop us from saying that Jesus is the 'son of God'?'

The Prophet [pbuh] replied: "These two things are not similar, because when we say Ibrahim [pbuh] is the *Khalil* of God, we mean something different. In reality, the word *Khalil* derives from *khillat* and *khillat*

---

[5] Please see glossary for more details.

means 'needliness and poverty'. So, he is called *Khalil* because he only needed God and he was totally cutoff from everything of the world, he only trusted God and only asked Him in time of need."

"And his story is that when his enemies decided to throw him in the fire and placed him on the catapult, God sent angel Gabriel [Jibreel] towards him and told Jibreel, "Go and help My servant." Jibreel went to Ibrahim [pbuh] and met him in air [while he was thrown towards fire] and told him, "Tell me what you want. God has sent me to help you." Ibrahim [pbuh] answered by saying, "No, I do not need your help. God is enough for me and I trust only Him. I will never ask anyone but Him. If I need anything, I will only ask Him." So, God called him *Khalil*, which means someone who is only needy of God, only depends on Him and is disconnected from everything other than Him and asking God only in time of his need. And if the meaning of *khillat* is taken as secrets then it means that he knew those secrets of God that no one else did, then *Khalil* would mean 'Knowledgeable of God' and 'Knowledgeable of His divine affairs' and on this basis, you cannot compare God to His creatures."

"Can you not see that when there is no need towards Him, then he cannot be *Khalil* and similarly, if the knowledge of His secrets does not exist, then he is again not a *Khalil*? But if a person has a son and he insults him or rejects his son, even then he cannot take him out of his fatherhood because birth is a reality. In addition, if God's said 'Ibrahim [pbuh] is My *Khalil*' based on this, it is incumbent upon you to call Prophet Isa [pbuh] His son, then it is also incumbent upon you to call Musa His son because he performed strange miracles that were different from those of Prophet Isa [pbuh]. Then, you will also have to say that Musa [pbuh] is His son and just like I told the Jews, you can also call Musa [pbuh] His leader, uncle, boss and master."

After hearing this, the Christians started saying to each other that it is written in the Holy Bible that Jesus said: 'Go towards my and your Father.'

The Prophet [pbuh] said: "If you practice what is written in this book [Bible, *Injeel*] and if it says, 'Go towards my and your Father,' then you will also have to say that all of those people to whom Prophet Isa [pbuh] was speaking to when he said this [sentence] are also God's sons and they were all God's sons on the same basis as Prophet Isa [pbuh] was God's son. And this quote from this book [Bible] falsifies your claim because you consider Prophet Isa [pbuh] as the son of God due to his special position and proximity to Him. Just now, you said that we call Prophet Isa [pbuh] son of God because of his special status that God has exclusively given him and not anyone else. And you are also aware of the fact that this special attribute was only possessed by Prophet Isa [pbuh] and not the ones to whom Prophet Isa [pbuh] said: 'Go towards my and your Father.'"

"Thus, this claim of yours that God made Prophet Isa [pbuh] His son because of his special attribute is falsified because 'being a son of God' is also proved for those who did not possess any special status. And is it not possible that you made a wrong interpretation and explanation of Prophet Isa's [pbuh] quote and made a mistake in understanding it? Because when he said: 'Go towards my and your Father' he might not have meant what you think."

"However, it is quite possible that he meant go towards your father [Adam or Noah [pbuh]] and very soon, God will ascend me towards them and gather me with them and 'Adam [pbuh] is my father, as well as yours.' Similarly, 'Noah [pbuh] is my father and also your father' [Noah [pbuh] is also called the second Adam [pbuh]] and it is possible that there might be another meaning to what he said which you cannot comprehend."

Upon hearing this, all the Christians were silent and said: 'We have never seen anyone [like Prophet Muhammad [pbuh]] who debates like this and we want to think over our matters.'

Part 3: Debate with Atheists

The Prophet [pbuh] then turned towards the atheists and said: "Now, tell me what is the reason behind your claim that the objects [or whatever is] in this Universe have no beginning and they have been there forever and will exist forever."

The atheists replied: 'We are simply stating what we observe. We have not seen *hudooth* [contingency, coming into existence] in objects [or whatever exists] of the Universe so we say that this Universe has been there forever and when we did not observe destruction and annihilation, we postulated that whatever exists in this Universe is not transient [will never annihilate].'

The Prophet [pbuh] said: "Did you find this Universe *qadeem* [eternally pre-existent, without a beginning] or did you find it eternal? If you say so, then explain if you yourself are in the same physical and intellectual state as you are now and that you will remain like this forever. If you will answer positively, then undoubtedly, you will deny your own observation and reject the observation of the observers [in other words, you yourself were not in the same physical and intellectual state]."

Facing this question from the Prophet [pbuh], the atheists replied: 'No, we do not find this Universe pre-existent or everlasting.'

The Prophet [pbuh] then said: "Then how come you said that the objects in this Universe are eternally pre-existent and eternal? And when you did not observe *hudooth* [contingency, coming into being] or *inqadha*⁶ (perishing, being transient) in this Universe, you called it pre-existent and eternal; while it was better for you, when you did not find eternal pre-existence and eternity in this Universe, to claim that this Universe is *haadith* [came into existence] and has *inqadha* (perishable). Alright, have you seen how the day and night come one after another?"

The atheists said: 'Yes.'

The Prophet [pbuh] said: "Do you think of the night and the day to be eternal?"

The atheists said: 'Yes.'

The Prophet [pbuh] said: "In your opinion, can the night and the day coexist?"

The atheists said: 'No.'

The Prophet [pbuh] continued: "Doesn't one of them separate from the other and come forward and the other one follow it?"

The atheists said: 'Yes, this is how it works.'

The Prophet [pbuh] said: "So, through your affirmation, you have said that the night and the day that have passed display *hudooth* [coming into existence], while you have not observed it directly. Now, tell me you say that the Universe is eternally pre-existent and not *haadith* [something pre-existent]. Do you know what are the things that you will have to admit to and reject, based on your proposition?"

The atheists said: 'Yes.'

---

⁶ Please see glossary for more details.

Chapter 1

The Prophet [pbuh] said: "You have definitely observed that in this Universe, one thing is dependent over another because existence of anything in this Universe is impossible without its contact [or connection] with another thing. You may have seen how some parts of a building are dependent over others or else, the building would be unstable and not be able to stand as a unit [will fall] and this is true for everything [in this Universe]. The same is true for all other objects. So, when these objects, while being eternally pre-existent, require other objects for their strength and completeness, so now tell me, what would have been their situation and characteristics had they been *haadith* [having a beginning]?"

Imam Ali [as] says that after hearing this question from Prophet Muhammad [pbuh], all the atheists were baffled and understood that it is impossible to acquire a new characteristic for a *haadith* object [something with a beginning] that is different from the characteristics of the objects which we call *qadeem* (eternally pre-existent).

The atheists stopped their discussion and said: 'We wish to think over our matters for some time...'

Chapter 1

Part 4: Debate with Dualists [*Sanaviyas*]

Prophet Muhammad [pbuh] then turned towards the *Sanaviyas* [Dualists, believers of two Gods], who believe that light [or goodness] and darkness [or evil] control the matters of this Universe.

The Prophet [pbuh] said: "Tell me what has forced you to claim that light and darkness control this Universe."

The Dualists replied: 'We have observed two discrete characteristics in this Universe, goodness and evil and we found out that these two are completely opposite of one another. So we could not accept that the one who does a good thing can also perform what is its opposite. Hence, we considered the performer of each one of these characteristics as a separate being. Can you not see that it is impossible for ice to be hot and fire to be cold? So we suggested two creators, the first one is light and the second one, darkness.'

The Prophet [pbuh] said: "Have you not observed blackness, whiteness, redness, yellowness and greenness and isn't each one of them opposite of the others? And that, just like how coldness and hotness cannot be together in one place, these colors can't be gathered in one place?" [meaning that these colors cannot be one other at the same time, e.g. green cannot be blue at the same time]

The Dualists replied: 'Yes.'

The Prophet [pbuh] said: "So, just like you have suggested one creator for every separate characteristic, can the creators of each one of these colors be considered separate?"

Everyone was silent when they heard this argument from Prophet Muhammad [pbuh].

The Prophet [pbuh] continued: "Now tell me, you say that light and darkness decide the affairs of this Universe together. How can light and darkness mix when it is the nature of lightness to ascend and the nature of darkness to descend? Can you not see that when a person walks towards east and another person walks towards west, is it possible for them to meet?"

The Dualists replied: 'No, it is impossible.'

The Prophet [pbuh] said: "Thus it is proved that light and darkness cannot be combined because each one of them moves in opposition to the other. When they cannot be combined together, they cannot be makers of Universe. So how do you think that the Universe is created by the combination of these two when combination of these elements is impossible? These two [light and darkness] are in fact the creatures of one God who intelligently prevails over them and wisely controls them."

The Dualists replied: 'Let us think about our views.'

Part 5: Debate with Polytheists

Then, the Prophet [pbuh] turned towards the Arab polytheists and said: "Why do you worship idols instead of worshipping Allah?"

The polytheists replied: 'We seek nearness to God through worshipping these idols.'

The Prophet [pbuh] said: "Can these idols hear? Do they obey their lord? Do they worship God so that you would become close to God by paying homage to them and their worship?"

The polytheists said: 'No, this is not so.'

The Prophet [pbuh] said: "You made these idols with your own hands so if worship was possible for them, it was them who should have worshipped you and not the other way around. In addition, the One who knows your needs and your future and knows your affairs has not ordered any such respect and homage to these idols…"

Upon hearing this, there was a discord among the polytheists. Some of them started saying that 'God incarnates himself in the bodies of few human beings and then we make the idols of these human beings and pay homage to them so that those statues in which our god was incarnated before will bring us closer to him.'

Others started saying that 'these idols were the sculptures of great servants of god who were obedient towards him. We made their idols so that they would be worshipped and in this way we openly show respect towards god.'

The last group among them said that 'when God created Adam [pbuh], He ordered the angels to prostrate before him while we were more worthy of prostrating before Adam than the angels and since we did not get the chance to do this, we made an idol of Adam and bowed before it so that we would achieve the same nearness to god just like the angels did.

And in the same way that you ordered your followers to prostrate towards the *Kaaba* [Holy Kaaba] in Mecca and you built mosques in other places and prostrated in those mosques but your intention was *Kaaba* and not the *mehrab* [the physical place of worship in mosque].

And even when you were prostrating towards *Kaaba*, your intention is not to prostrate to the *Kaaba* itself but to prostrate to God. Our intentions too, are directed towards worship of God while seemingly we are prostrating the idols.'

The Prophet [pbuh] said: "You are on the wrong path and misguided. By saying this, you are attributing the characteristics of the creatures to the Creator because when your god will incarnate himself in an object [or body], then that object will surround him."

"Then, if so, what difference will remain between this God who incarnates himself in an object and the things which mix [or combine] with other things [having characteristics] such as color, odor, softness, hardness, lightness and heaviness?"

"And why should these objects [in which God incarnates] be considered *haadith* [contingent, with a beginning] and God *qadeem* [eternally pre-existent]? [means that it is opposite and impossible as these objects are created and have a beginning while God is pre-existent, without a beginning]."

Chapter 1

"Why don't we then call God *haadith* and take these bodies *qadeem*? And also, tell me how can God be in need of space when He was there before the creation of space itself and when you attributed the characteristic of *hulool*[7] (incarnation) to God and added the characteristics of creatures to him. Then it is necessary for you to also place the characteristic of *zawaal*[8] (transient, falling) in Him. After that, for the one who has the characteristic of *zawaal*, you must also add the characteristic of *fana*[9] (destruction) to it."

"This is because all of these characteristics are indispensable for those who incarnate and also for the objects in which others incarnate. And it is definite that all of these objects are variant [have tendency to change over time]. So if God does not change after *hulool*, it would mean that an invariant thing will be simultaneously moving and stationary, will be black and white, and red and yellow at the same time which is impossible."

"And it is also proven that when something [such as an object] acquires the characteristics of a *haadith* [with a beginning], it itself transforms into a *haadith* object. And you have no choice but to admit that my God is superior to all of these *haadith* characteristics [of creatures]. And when the claim that 'God incarnates in someone' is itself proven false, then the entire belief system which rests upon it is also falsified."

Upon hearing this, all of them were silent and said: 'We would like to think upon their beliefs.'

Then, the Prophet [pbuh] turned towards the second group and said: "Now tell me, when you worship the sculptures [statues] of those

---

[7] Please see glossary for more details.
[8] Please see glossary for more details.
[9] Please see glossary for more details.

human beings who used to worship God and when you prostrate before them and put your pure foreheads on the ground, then tell me what ways of expressing servitude have you specifically reserved for the One who is the Lord of these statues and is the Lord of the Worlds you have discarded? Do you not know that you are not supposed to equate the One who is worthy of respect and worship with His servants and creatures?"

"Suppose you show same level of respect and glorification to a king or an important person as you show to his servant; would this not be considered as an insult and humiliation to the King or that important person?"

The polytheists replied: 'Yes, this would be so.'

The Prophet [pbuh] said: "So are you not aware that by bowing, respecting and glorifying the sculptures of the obedient servants of God, you are in fact insulting God?" [because then it seems that there is no better way of expressing servitude towards God]

Upon hearing this, they were silent and said: 'We would like to think over our beliefs.'

The Prophet [pbuh] then turned towards the third group and said: "You gave my example and compared me to you while in reality we are not equal. We are God's servants, His creatures and nurtured by Him and we do as He says and avoid what He has forbidden and worship Him the way He wishes us to worship Him. When He orders us to do something, we do not go after something against that order which He has not permitted us to do because we do not know and it might be possible that He wishes us to do an action but not the other one which He has forbidden us. He has forbidden us to transgress His order. So when God ordered us to worship Him while facing the *Kaaba*, we exactly followed His order. And when He ordered us to face *Kaaba* even when we were in other cities, we again did what He had ordered and we never tried to go beyond what He had asked us to do. So when God ordered the prostration before Adam, He did not order the prostration before Adam's [pbuh] sculpture [which is separate and different from Adam]. It was obligatory upon you to obey this order of God and not compare it [using analogy] to Sculpture of Adam [pbuh]. How do you know that maybe God will not like this deed of yours when He has not ordered such a thing? You must be observing this in your daily life that a person invites you to his house. Is it possible then that you enter his house on another day without his permission or go to another one of his houses? Or suppose that a person provides you his clothes, food and animal for travel, will you take these things next time without his permission?"

The polytheists said: 'No.'

The Prophet [pbuh] said: "Alright, if you don't take these things but take his other belongings which are of the same colour, shape etc., will that be right?"

The polytheists said: 'No, because he did not give us permission.'

The Prophet [pbuh] said: "Alright, so tell me, is God more worthy of the fact that no one commits something against His orders in His kingdom or His servants [creatures]?"

The polytheists said: 'God is more worthy of the fact that no one acts against His orders in this world.'

The Prophet [pbuh] said: "Then why do you do this [worship idols]? When did God ask you to worship these idols?"

After hearing this, they were all silent and said: 'We would like to think over our beliefs.'

Imam al-Sadiq [as] says that Imam Ali [as] said: 'By God not even three days had passed that all those 25 scholars who came for debate, and were five individuals from each sect, converted to Islam. They declared: 'O Muhammad! Until today we never heard such solid arguments and proofs which you presented to us. And we declare that you are the Prophet of God."

These debates of Prophet Muhammad [pbuh] were reported by Imam Ja'far al-Sadiq [as] through his grandfather Imam Zayn al-Abedin [as] who reported from Imam Ali [as] who was with Prophet Muhammad [pbuh] when the scholars of five religions [Christianity, Judaism, Atheism, Dualism and Polytheism] came to see him and challenged him.

Reference: *al-Ihtajaj*, **vol. 1, p. 27-44 [written by al-Allama Abu Mansur Ahmed Ibn Ali al-Tabarsi. d. 599 A.H.**

Chapter 2

Debate of Prophet [pbuh] with a group of Polytheists

It is reported from Imam Abu Muhammad Hasan al-Askari [as]: 'I asked my father Ali Ibn Muhammad [as]: 'Did Prophet of God [pbuh] do any debates with Jews and Polytheists?' **He replied:** 'Yes, several times."

Then he [as] said: 'Once Prophet of God [pbuh] was sitting on the floor around the Holy *Kaaba*. The companions were around him. He [pbuh] was teaching them the Book of Allah and divine command about good and forbidden actions. A group of leaders of Quraysh including Walid Ibn Mughayra al-Makhzoumi, Abul Bakhtari bin Hisham, Abu Jahal, 'Aas Ibn Wael Sahmi, and Abudullah Ibn Umayyah al-Makhzoumi came there. They started talking to each other saying: 'Muhammad's activities are increasing day by day and the number of followers is becoming larger. It is better we should have a debate with him and prove his views false so that his prophetic mission gets belittled in front of his followers, he loses his respect and gets humiliated. Perhaps, he gives up his heretic, rebellious, misguiding and false beliefs. Otherwise we will use our bloody sword to stop him.'

Abu Jahal: 'But who will talk to Muhammad and debate with him?'

Ibn Abi Umayyah: 'I will debate with him. I am equal to him in tribal rivalry, and I am qualified enough to debate and discuss with him.'

Abu Jahal: 'Okay.'

Then all these influential figures of Quraysh approached Prophet Muhammad [pbuh] and the discussion began.

Ibn Abi Umayyah: 'O Muhammad! You have made a great claim and uttered very horrific statements. You imagine that you are a messenger of God. However, it is not worthy of God to make a man like us His messenger. You eat like we eat, you drink like we drink, and you go to markets like we do. Similarly, these kings of Rome and these kings of Persia make their messengers those who are wealthy, and have material greatness, those who have great palaces, houses and tents, have many slaves and servants. God of the worlds is even greater than these kings are His slaves, and if you were the Prophet of God, then you would have similar greatness [like God] and you had an angel with you who would verify your statements, and we could have seen that angel.

And if God wished to send a Prophet towards us, he would not be a human being, but would send an angel as his Prophet who would not be a human like us.

O Muhammad you look like bewitched person and do not look like a Prophet.'

Prophet of God [pbuh]: "Do you want say something more?"

Ibn Abi Umayyah: 'Yes! If God wished to send a messenger towards us, He would have made such a person His messenger who would be at higher status than us wealth and greatness. So this Qur'an about which you think has descended upon you, could it not have descended upon great individuals in Mecca and Medina, for example, Walid Ibn Mughayra from Mecca, Urwa bin Masu'd Thaqafi from Ta'ef?'

Prophet of God [pbuh]: "Did you finish your talk?"

Chapter 2

Ibn Abi Umayyah: 'No. We will not believe in you until you bring out springs in the land of Mecca because the terrain of Mecca is rocky and mountainous. You cut and dig the land of Mecca and bring out springs from it because we need it.

Or we will believe in you if you own a garden of grapes and dates. You eat from it and also give us to eat from it. And streams of water should flow in between these gardens.

Or you bring down heavens upon us or bring God and angels before us and they should be face to face with us, or you should have a house of gold and you should give us from it, or you climb to heaven and this climbing is not enough, we will believe in you only when you bring down a book upon us, that we can read and it should have my name and my companions names in it from God whereby it should be mentioned in it that you should believe in Muhammad bin Abdullah, he is my prophet and you should confirm his words, because whatever he says is from us. In spite of all this O Muhammad we cannot be sure to give you our word that we will believe in you or not. And suppose even you climb up in the heavens and open its doors and let us in there, even then it is possible that we can say you have blindfolded us with your magic and bewitched us.'

Prophet of God [pbuh]: "Is there anything more left of your word?"

Ibn Abi Umayyah: 'O Muhammad! Aren't these arguments that I have brought forth and criticisms against you enough and does it leave room for more? Now you can say whatever you like and explain about yourself and if you have logical reasons, then answer our questions.'

Prophet of God [pbuh]: "O Lord! You hear every sound and You know everything and whatever your servants say, You know it very well."

Right at that time, following verses of Qur'an were revealed:

And they say: What is the matter with this Messenger that he eats food and goes about in the markets; why has not an angel been sent down to him, so that he should have been a warner with him?. Or (why is not) a treasure sent down to him, or he is made to have a garden from which he should eat? And the unjust say: You do not follow any but a man deprived of reason. See what likenesses they apply to you, so they have gone astray; therefore they shall not be able to find a way. Blessed is He Who, if He please, will give you what is better than this, gardens beneath which rivers flow, and He will give you palaces. [25: 7-10]

Then, it may be that you will give up part of what is revealed to you and your breast will become straitened by it because they say: Why has not a treasure been sent down upon him or an angel come with him? You are only a warner; and Allah is custodian over all things. [11: 12]

And they say: Why has not an angel been sent down to him? And had We sent down an angel, the matter would have certainly been decided and then they would not have been respited. [6: 8]

The Prophet of God [pbuh] then said: "O Ibn Abi Umayyah!, You have said that I eat in the same manner as you eat and for this very reason I shouldn't be the messenger of God. So listen this is the matter of God Himself. He orders whatever He wishes. You and others have no right to criticize and raise argument on this matter. Don't you see how He keeps few individuals as poor and needy and makes few others rich and wealthy, bestows respect to few and humiliates others, some are healthy while others are sick? Some are honorable and others are lower status, and among there is no one who doesn't eat food, and it is not allowed for poor to complaint to God: 'Why did you make us poor? And made others wealthy?' And weak have no right to ask God:

'Why have you made us low and made other honorable? And similarly disabled and weak have no right to complain to God: 'Why have You made us disabled and weak while You have bestowed others with health?' And those who are humiliated cannot say: 'Why have You humiliated us and bestowed others with greatness?' And similarly those who are ugly cannot say: 'Why have You made us ugly and bestowed others with beauty?'"

"And if they [all of the above] say such to [complain to] God, it will be as if they would criticize God and will thus dispute with God and become infidels. And even if they say it, God will reply to them: 'I am the greatest King, the ultimate humiliate and bestower of greatness, the one makes rich, makes poor, bestower of respect, and the one disgraces, bestower of health, makes sick, and you all are my servants and there is no way for you all except to accept my decree and be happy with my judgment. And if you bow down to my orders then you will be included among my believing servants. And if you disobey then you will be counted among infidels."

"Now your saying that 'King of Rome and King of Persia make their messengers only those who are wealthy, and have material greatness, those who have great palaces, houses and tents, have many slaves and servants. God of the worlds is even greater than these kings are His slaves, and so if you were the Prophet of God, then you would have all these things…"

"So the reality is that God is the al-Wise Planner and He doesn't act according to your whims and imaginations; instead He orders and acts on whatever He wishes."

"O Ibn Abi Umayyah! God has sent His Prophet only so that he preaches people the knowledge of His religion and invite them towards their God and tolerate hardships and difficulties day and night for preaching His message. So if the Prophet lived in palace then his servants and slaves will keep him hidden and separated from people. So [in this situation] will not the purpose of His messengership be lost and the matters be delayed and become difficult? Don't you see that when King becomes hidden from the eyes of people, then how the corruption appears and problems creep up in the society while they are not aware of it."

"O Ibn Abi Umayyah! God has made me Prophet and sent me and you are seeing that I don't have material possessions and wealth and this is because He wants to show you His power and authority. He is the supporter of His Prophet and you people don't have power to murder him and prevent him from propagation of truth and this is the manifest proof of His power and your helplessness. And soon God will bestow me victory over you people and then I will kill some of you and will take some others of you as prisoners. Then God will bless me with victory over your cities and then those who will rule over your cities will not be from you and will be against your religion [believers]."

The Prophet of God [pbuh] then continued...

"And your saying that 'If you were the Prophet of God, then there would have been an angel with you, who would testify you and we would be able to see him. Rather if God sent a Prophet towards us, He wouldn't send a human being like us; instead, He would have sent an angel as His Prophet.'"

"So listen! An angel cannot be seen by your eyes and sensed your senses. And if power of your sight is increased and then you see an angel, even then you will say 'this is not an angel, it is a human being' because it has appeared to you in the physical form and whenever it will come in physical form, it will appear in the form of a human being so that you can become familiar to it, listen what it says, understand purpose of his talk. Then how will you verify truthfulness of angel and testify whatever he said is right?"

"It is for the same reason that God has made human being as His Prophet [and not an angel] and showed miracles and wonders through his hands which other human beings cannot show so for this reason people like you believe in their truthfulness and in the fact that they are sent by God."

"And if He had sent angel as prophet and miracles and wonders were seen through him, then you by assuming that showing these miracles and wonders is inherent in all the angels and that these great feats are a part of their nature wouldn't consider their 'miracles' as 'miracles'. Don't you see birds that they fly and you do not call their 'flying' as miracle? Why? Because flying is a part of their nature and inherent to them. But if a human being starts flying then you will call it as miracle. So this is a grace of God that [in this way] He has made this matter easier so that it is easy for you to believe and that His argument prevails over you."

The Prophet of God [pbuh] then continued...

"And your saying that I am a 'bewitched man'; so it is really regrettable that you have said it about me while you know very well that I am more intelligent and wiser than you and since my birth until today while I am forty years of age, have you ever seen me committing a lowly act ? or found me disgraceful ? or seen me lying ? or found me deceitful ? or found an error in my word ? or an irrationality in my opinions ? Can you rationally accept this fact that a person can remain in this condition for such a long duration only on the basis of his personal ability and power? or can he be protected from all the evils [and imperfections] by the power of God and His might?"

"And your saying that 'if this Qur'an was to descend, it should have descended upon two great rich personalities of Mecca or Ta'ef such as Walid and Urwa.' So you should know that the way you feel about the material possessions of this world, God does take it that way. While the worldly possessions have high value in your eyes, in the eyes of God, these have no value. Instead, if in the view of God, this world had value equal to the wing of a mosquito, then the nonbeliever wouldn't be able to drink even a mouthful of water from it."

"And God's distribution [of blessings] has nothing to do with you. Instead with His benevolence and mercy, He blesses among his servants to whom He wishes and whatever He wishes He does it. And He is not of those who are afraid like you who is afraid of wealth and possessions of rich individuals and consider it as a sign of prophethood. Neither is He from among those who have greed towards wealth and possessions like you, who is greedy and wants to specially keep wealth bound to prophethood. And He is not among those who are after their inordinate desires like you are after your pleasures and keeps that ahead which doesn't deserve to be kept ahead. Without any doubt His deal is on the basis of justice and fairness and He doesn't prefer anyone and bestow honor in religion and His greatness except to one who is most obedient to Him and most superior in serving Him."

"And similarly His doesn't push anyone back in honor and preference in religion and greatness except the one who has drifted far away from his obedience to Him. By all means, He never looks at anyone's personality, He never cares about the wealth and worldly possessions as these possessions are bestowed to them by His own benevolence to them. And remember when He bestows wealth and worldly possessions to someone, it is not obligatory for Him to bless him with prophethood because no one can force Him to act against what He wishes."

"Don't you see that how He has made one person wealthy and gave him ugly face and made another person very poor and gave him beautiful face. Blessed one with honor but kept him poor. Blessed one with wealth but didn't give him honor. Then the ugly faced wealthy cannot say that O God with wealth also make me beautiful like that person, and neither that beautiful person can say that [O God] with beauty bless me with wealth like that person and nor honorable person, with his honor can also ask for wealth and nor that lowly wealthy person with his wealth can also ask for honor like that honorable person. This is not possible except for the order of God Who has distributed all this with His decree. And He is All-Wise in His actions, all-Praiseworthy in His deeds and this is what He, the All-exalted has said "I have not descended this Qur'an except on a man from two great cities." and God has said: "Isn't it the mercy of Your Lord O Muhammad! That We have distributed among them their earnings for life of this world in such a way that We have given preference to some of them over others in some aspects, thus some of them will need others for wealth, while one will need other for their comfort, and for services."

"That's why you see that the great Kings and very wealthy individuals are also needy like the poorest because the worldly possessions that this one has that poor one doesn't have it; the services that that poorest person can provide, this king cannot and so to acquire knowledge and wisdom, rich is forced to seek the help of poor."

"So this poor person needs the wealth of rich King and the King is needy of knowledge, counsel and wisdom of this poor man. Thus it is neither appropriate for the King to say that I wish I could also have knowledge of this poor man and nor is it appropriate for the poor man with knowledge and wise counsel to also desire for the wealth of King and wish to use both his artful wisdom and also control the wealth of the King."

The Prophet of God [pbuh] then continued…

"But your saying that 'We will not believe in you until you bring out streams of water in Mecca because the land of Mecca is rocky mountainous. You cut out its land and dig it and make channels of water in it because we direly need it.' You have demanded this from while in reality you are totally ignorant of the logic of God behind it.

O Ibn Abi Umayyah! Suppose if you are able to do all this, will you then become Prophet?"

Ibn Abi Umayyah: 'No'

Prophet of God [pbuh]: "Have you seen Ta'ef where your gardens exist? Wasn't the land barren, rocky and unsuitable for cultivation that you plowed, made its bumpy terrain smooth and brought out streams of water from it?"

Ibn Abi Umayyah: 'Yes'

Prophet of God [pbuh]: "Is this type of work done by other people too?"

Ibn Abi Umayyah: 'Yes'

Prophet of God [pbuh]: "Then have you and all of them become prophets?"

Ibn Abi Umayyah: 'No'

Prophet of God [pbuh]: "Then when these things cannot be proof of your prophethood so how can these things be proof of Muhammad's Prophethood? And what you said earlier is same as if you say that we will not believe in you as Prophet until you do not stand up as common people stand up and do not walk as common people walk and do not eat as common people eat. And your saying that 'You should have a garden of grapes and dates from which you yourself eat and also give us to eat from it.' So don't you and your friends own gardens of grapes and dates in Ta'ef from which you all eat and also give to others? Thus, because of these gardens have you all become Prophets?"

Ibn Abi Umayyah: 'No'

Prophet of God [pbuh]: "Then what is your condition that you are demanding such things that if they do exist even then the truthfulness and authenticity of a matter cannot be proved; instead if these are used as an argument to prove authenticity, then it will amount to nothing but lie and deceit. Because it would mean that to prove something, an argument was used which in reality was false and baseless and doesn't deserve to be called as a proof; and its aim was nothing but to cheat and deceive common ignorant people and misguide them. And Prophet of God is loftier and dignified than this [act of deceit and cheating]."

The Prophet of God [pbuh] then continued…

"And now your saying that heavens should fall upon us; so the reality is that if heaven falls on you that you will be doomed and you will die then your real motive behind this demand will be that you want Prophet of God to kill you while in reality the Prophet of God is much more merciful and compassionate towards you than [wishing to] kill you and he has not come to this world to kill. Instead he wants to establish proofs of God upon you. And the proofs of God are never in harmony for a Prophet to establish over servants of God. Because servants of God [people] are not aware of the corrective and corruptive issues and there is a great variation in their dispositions and natures which makes agreement on one thing impossible [one person wants something while other doesn't]. God is your physician and He doesn't say something which is impossible. Have you seen a physician who gives medicine according to the wish of patients? What he thinks he does it whether they are happy or unhappy. Similarly God is your physician so if you will use His recommended medicine, you will be cured and if you refuse taking it, you will continue to suffer from the disease."

"Now your saying that 'Until you bring God and angels face to face with us so that we can see them, we will not believe.' So this is totally impossible demand which is not hidden from anyone. Remember that my God in not like creatures that He comes and goes, moves, and comes face to face with a thing that we can bring Him. So it proves that your demand is impossible to fulfill. And in reality what you have demanded about My Lord is more deserving for your idols because all these qualities are present in your weak and imperfect idols who cannot hear, cannot see, neither have they had knowledge of anything, nor they can give you anything, or to others."

"O Ibn Abi Umayyah! Don't you own property and gardens in Ta'ef and Mecca and don't you keep your representatives over it?"

Chapter 2

Ibn Abi Umayyah: 'Why not?'

Prophet of God [pbuh]: "So do you handle the matters personally by yourself or you do it via your 'representatives' who act on your behalf between you and the second party and make deal with them?"

Ibn Abi Umayyah: 'Through representatives'

Prophet of God [pbuh]: "If sometimes those who do business with you, your tenants and your servants, demand your representatives that we will not accept you as representative until you do not bring Ibn Abi Umayyah to us, so that we can see him and whatever you told us attributing to him, we would hear that directly from him. So would you allow it to happen and would you take this as reasonable from them?"

Ibn Abi Umayyah: 'No'

Prophet of God [pbuh]: "So in the same way as your representatives should have a 'specific sign' that would point to your representation by them, isn't it obligatory upon people to testify them?" [that they are your representatives]

Ibn Abi Umayyah: 'Why not?'

Prophet of God [pbuh]: "Is it possible that when your representatives listen to that 'demand' they come to you and say 'You come with us because they are demanding that you go to them' So won't you be offended by this action of your representative and will not you say to him that you are my 'messenger' neither advisor and nor ruler."

Ibn Abi Umayyah: 'Yes'

Prophet of God [pbuh]: "Then why do you ask from the messenger of the God of Worlds that he would keep an abominable relationship that he would order His Lord to do something and prevent Him from doing something while you do not allow even your ordinary representatives to give you any type of order."

The Prophet [pbuh] then said: "By these solid arguments from me, all what you said and your claims are refuted and your criticisms are rebutted.

And your saying that 'If you were Prophet, you would have owned a golden palace' So you know that Pharaohs of Egypt had similar palaces. Thus, did they become prophets by having these grand decorated palaces?"

Ibn Abi Umayyah: 'No'

Prophet of God [pbuh]: "So in the same way this thing cannot be a proof of my prophethood. And your saying that until you climb up in the heavens and until you bring down a written book for us, we will not believe in you. So O Ibn Abi Umayyah! Climbing up to the heavens is more difficult than bringing down something from it. And you have already said that even if you climb over heaven, we will not believe you and similarly you have said that even after the book descends from the heaven we may believe or it is possible that we may not believe. So O Ibn Abi Umayyah! In this situation when you are obstinately adherent to your disbelief and arrogance, then your cure is nothing but that you should suffer punishment at the hands of friends of God [*Awliya Allah*] and His angels. God has blessed me with *Hikmatal Balighatal Jamiah*[10] (Ultimate and Complete Wisdom) through which all your false arguments and criticisms are refuted."

---

[10] Please see glossary for more details.

Abu Jahal: 'O Muhammad ! Is it not so that when *Bani Israel* [the nation of Prophet Musa [pbuh]] demanded from Musa [pbuh] to make them see God, they were punished with thunder from sky?'

Prophet of God [pbuh]: "Yes, it did."

Abu Jahal: 'So if you are really the Prophet of God, then descend the punishment of thunder from sky upon us because what we have demanded is more severe [in deserving punishment] than the nation of Musa [pbuh]. They had said to Musa [pbuh] to show God and we are saying that we will not believe until you bring God and His angels in front of us so that we can see them.'

Prophet of God [pbuh]: "O Abu Jahal! Are you not aware of the story of Ibrahim *Khalil Allah* [pbuh] when he was elevated into the *malakut* [heavens, hidden world], as the God says: '*And thus did We show Ibrahim the kingdom of the heavens and the earth and that he might be of those who are sure.*'[Qur'an, 6:75]. So when he was elevated to the heavens, He made powerful his sight and thus whatever was open and secret on earth became visible to him. So when he saw a man and a woman committing fornication, he prayed to curse them and so they died. Then he saw two others in the same condition [committing fornication], he prayed to curse them and they too died. Then he again saw two others in the same condition and so he prayed again to curse them and they too died. Then he again saw two others in the same condition and when he wanted to pray to curse them, God sent revelation upon him: 'O Ibrahim! Stop your prayers to curse my servants and maids; For I am Forgiving, Merciful, Al-Mighty and Tolerant God. In the same way as their worship doesn't give Me any benefit, their sins also do not harm Me. And so when I punish them it is not meant to satisfy My anger over them like you have done. So now you should hold your cursing prayers from my servants; for you are only My warning servant. Do not try to become My partner in my Kingdom. Do not try to prevail over Me and My servants. Remember that I deal with My servants in three ways:

[1]. If they repent, then I accept their repentance and forgive their sins and cover their faults.

[2]. If they do not repent even then I keep away my punishment from them because I know that their progeny will have virtuous believers and so because of these believers who will be born, I show mercy towards their father and mothers until when these believers are born, and then I tighten My grip on their fathers and mothers with my punishment and tribulations and,

[3]. O Ibrahim! When they neither repent nor they have any believer in their progeny, then even much more than your wish is My great punishment descends upon them because My punishment over My servants is to the level of My Magnificence and My Greatness."

"O Ibrahim! Do not come in between Me and My servants because I am more merciful to them than you. I am the Almighty, Tolerant, All-Knowing and Al-Wise God. With My Knowledge I make My plans for them and I implement upon them My decisions with My power.'"

Prophet of God [pbuh] then said: "O Abu Jahal! Certainly the divine punishment is away from you because He knows that a virtuous son Akramah will be born from you; otherwise the divine punishment would have descended upon you and those who are like you among Quraysh and this respite from God is only for the fact that a few among you will believe in Muhammad [pbuh] in near future and will be prosperous in both the worlds. Thus God doesn't wish to deprive them of this great felicity; and some of them are such that pure and virtuous progeny will appear from them and so He is waiting for them to appear.

If this wasn't the fact, the divine punishment would have descended upon you much earlier. And now you look at the sky."

And when he [pbuh] looked at the sky, the doors of heaven opened and fire started descending down and it reached very near over the heads of those who were present until they felt its heat. Abu Jahal and others present there started feeling stressed and were gripped in the state of fear.

Then the Prophet of God [pbuh] said: "Don't be afraid. God doesn't want to kill you. He showed you this to give a warning."

Reference: *al-Ihtajaj*, **vol. 1, p. 47-67** [written by al-Allama Abu Mansur Ahmed Ibn Ali al-Tabarsi. d. 599 A.H.]

Chapter 3

Prophet's [pbuh] debate with a group of Jews

Imam Hassan Askari [as] said: 'When Prophet [pbuh] was living in Mecca, God's order was such that while offering his prayers, he should face *Bayt–ul–Muqaddas* [the holy al-Aqsa mosque in Jerusalem] and when possible, keep *Kaaba* [the Holy *Kaaba*] in between the *Bayt–ul–Muqaddas* and Mecca and when this was not possible, keep *Bayt–ul–Muqaddas* as *Qibla* [direction to which Muslims turn for their prayers] and this routine continued for 13 years.

When Prophet [pbuh] migrated to Medina, he would still face *Bayt–ul–Muqaddas*, while praying [a direction] that deviated from *Kaaba*, and this continued for about 16 or 17 months.

After seeing this, extremist and mischievous Jews[11] said that how strange it is that Muhammad [pbuh] faces our *Qibla* while praying and he has adopted our ways and style in his prayers.

When the Prophet [pbuh] found out about what the Jews had been saying, he was hurt and severely grieved; it bothered him to pray while

---

[11]Three tribes of Jews lived in strong forts in Medina at that time: *Banu Qurayza, Banu Nudhayr* and *Banu Qaynqa'*. They were bitter enemies of Prophet Muhammad [pbuh] and Muslims. They broke their pledge with Prophet [pbuh] and started a campaign of propaganda and insult against Prophet [pbuh] and Muslims. They conspired to kill Prophet [pbuh] and Muslims and waged war against Muslims either directly or indirectly by supporting other tribes. Ultimately, all these three tribes were banished from Medina. For more details see the book, *The Message,* by Ayatullah Ja'far Subhani available at: http://www.al-islam.org/message/

facing their *Qibla* and he wished to make *Kaaba* his *Qibla*. As soon as he wished this, Jibreel came to him.

The Prophet [pbuh] said to Jibreel: "If God changed *Qibla* from *Bayt–ul–Muqaddas* to *Kaaba*, I would be very pleased because it hurts me to hear what the Jews are saying about praying while facing their *Qibla*."

Jibreel [a] replied: 'Oh Prophet of God! Ask God for changing the *Qibla* and I am sure that God will not reject your wish and request.' Upon hearing this, the Prophet [pbuh] prayed to God. As soon as he prayed, Jibreel went to Heavens and returned immediately.

He said: 'Oh Muhammad [pbuh]! Recite this:

Indeed We see the turning of your face to heaven, so We shall surely turn you to a qibla which you shall like; turn then your face towards the Sacred Mosque, and wherever you are, turn your face towards it, and those who have been given the Book most surely know that it is the truth from their Lord; and Allah is not at all heedless of what they do.

And even if you bring to those who have been given the Book every sign they would not follow your qibla, nor can you be a follower of their qibla, neither are they the followers of each other's qibla, and if you follow their desires after the knowledge that has come to you, then you shall most surely be among the unjust. [2:144-145][12]

Upon hearing this, the Jews said: 'Why did Muslims stop facing their previous *Qibla* [*Bayt–ul–Muqaddas*] and turned to *Kaaba*?'

God gave a perfect answer to this question and the **Prophet [pbuh] said:**

---

[12] For exegesis of these ayahs, please see *Tafsir al-Mizan* available online at: http://www.shiasource.com/al-mizan/ See under verse 2:144

"The fools among the people will say: What has turned them from their qibla which they had? Say: The East and the West belong only to Allah; He guides whom He likes to the right path. [2:142].

And He is all-aware of the interests of His servants, and it is He who will send His obedient servants to gardens of bliss."[13]

Imam Hassan Askari [as] said: 'Then, some Jews came to the Prophet [pbuh] and started talking: 'O Muhammad! You prayed while facing the *Qibla* you call *Bayt–ul–Muqaddas* for 14 years and now you suddenly left it so can we ask you a question: Were you following *haq* [righteous way, truth] before and now you have left it and started following *batil* [erroneous way, wrong, against *haq*] or were you following *batil* before for a period of time and now you have come to follow *haq*?'

The Prophet [pbuh] said: "I was on *haq* before and I am on *haq* now as well because God's clear command is that the east and the west are His and He guides whoever He wishes to the right path."

"Oh servants of God! When Allah felt that your interest and welfare lies in praying while facing the east, He ordered you to make east your *Qibla* and when He saw that your interest and welfare lies in making

---

[13] Related verses of Holy Qur'an: *And thus We have made you a medium (just) nation that you may be the bearers of witness to the people and (that) the Messenger may be a bearer of witness to you; and We did not make that which you would have to be the qibla but that We might distinguish him who follows the Messenger from him who turns back upon his heels, and this was surely hard except for those whom Allah has guided aright; and Allah was not going to make your faith to be fruitless; most surely Allah is Affectionate, Merciful to the people* [2-143]. *And from whatsoever place you come forth, turn your face towards the Sacred Mosque; and surely it is the very truth from your Lord, and Allah is not at all heedless of what you do. And from whatsoever place you come forth, turn your face towards the Sacred Mosque; and wherever you are turn your faces towards it, so that people shall have no accusation against you, except such of them as are unjust; so do not fear them, and fear Me, that I may complete My favor on you and that you may walk on the right course* [2:149-150].

the west as your *Qibla*, He ordered you to face the west. Hence, do not interfere in divine plans for His servants and His will for your interest"

The Prophet [pbuh] then continued: "Now you tell me, you stopped working on Saturdays and then you worked on all the days. Then again you stopped working on Saturdays and then you again worked on all the days. Now tell me, did you come towards *batil* from *haq* or from *batil* towards *haq* or from *batil* towards *batil* or from *haq* towards *haq*? Explain in any way you wish. Then our answer will be the same as yours."

The Jews said: 'Yes, our *'tark al-amal'* [leaving daily work for earning] on Saturdays was *haq* and our working afterwards was also *haq*.'

The Prophet [pbuh] said: "So, this is exactly our situation. It was *haq* at that time when *Bayt–ul–Muqaddas* was made the *Qibla*. Then, the decision to make *Kaaba* the new *Qibla* at that time was also *haq*."

The Jews said: 'Has *bada*[14] (change) occurred in Lord when He ordered you to turn your face from *Bayt–ul–Muqaddas* towards *Kaaba* while praying?'

The Prophet [pbuh] said: "This change in the *Qibla* cannot lead to *bada* in God. The truth is that He is aware of all the consequences. He is omnipotent over the advantages and benefits [of His orders]. He cannot make mistakes nor can anyone change His decisions. God is higher over all these things."

Then the Prophet said to them: "Oh Jews! Tell me, does not God give a person a disease and then cure him? And He cures him and does He

---

[14] Please see glossary for more details.

not give him an incurable disease? Is this *bada* for God? And is it not so that God gives life and takes it away? Does this lead to *bada* for God?"

The Jews replied: 'No.'

The Prophet [pbuh] said: "Then just like this, God's Prophet Muhammad [pbuh] prayed facing the *Kaaba* while before, he used to pray facing *Bayt-ul-Muqaddas*. So, no *bada* occurred by His first order [so that there would be the necessity to give a new order] but that what happened was the need of time and the need of time changes in every era."

He [pbuh] continued: "Does not God bring winter after summer and summer after winter and does this change in seasons manifest *bada* in God's decision?"

The Jews said: 'No.'

The Prophet [pbuh] said: "Then similarly, no *bada* occurred with the change of *Qibla*."

He [pbuh] then said: "Has not God ordered us to wear thick and warm clothes in winter to protect ourselves from cold and in summer, to protect our bodies from the heat of summer? Then, wasn't the order given in summer against the order given in winter? So is this contradiction tantamount to *bada*?"

The Jews replied: 'No.'

The Prophet [pbuh] said: "Similarly, God gives you an order and it is in your interests. Then, at another time, He gives you a different order while keeping in view your interests. And then, when you will obey Him in both the situations, you will deserve His reward."

Then he [pbuh] said: "Oh servants of God! Think this way as if you are sick and the Lord of the world is your physician. So, the interest and welfare of the patients lies in acting upon the advice of physician. And not in considering the patients' desires and fulfilling their wants. Thus, submit to Allah's orders so that you will be among those who are successful."

Reference: *al-Ihtajaj*, **vol. 1, p. 81-86 [written by al-Allama Abu Mansur Ahmed Ibn Ali al-Tabarsi. d. 599 A.H.]**

Glossary of key terms

bada *[revealing after concealing]* *Bada* is an Islamic concept regarding Allah's will. Based on some specific circumstances, Allah [swt] reveals His will opposite to what was expected. Muslims were accused by the Jews that they believe that Allah [swt] is ignorant of the ultimate outcome (God forbid) of His orders. This accusation can be defended by the fact that Allah is the Ultimate Wise and creatures or people are ignorant of Allah's will and not that the Allah [swt] is ignorant.

fanaa [destruction, annihilation] *Fanaa* is the term used for "dissolution" or "annihilation". The term refers to the end of this world. Everything which is created is dependent upon the Creator for its survival and will undergo destruction before the Day of Judgment. *Fanaa* is thus an inherent characteristic of all created things which would get destructed except Allah [swt].

haadith [contingent, that which comes into being] *Haadith* is an object which didn't exist once and then came into the existence. Thus every object in the universe is attributed to this quality because it came into existence. Every *haadith* needs external factor for coming into being, time and space. As Allah [swt] being totally independent and beyond time and space cannot be attributed to be *haadith*. Any god other than Allah [swt] is in fact not god and is *haadith*.

hikmatal balighatal jamiah [Ultimate and Complete Wisdom] This term refers to a high level of wisdom which is ultimate and comprehensive. It is greater than the knowledge itself which is just to collect random information. The word *Hikmat* is derived from *Hakamah* which is a tool to stop the horse from indulgence. A person having such wisdom is always careful in his thoughts, speech, ideas, acts etc. The words and the speeches of Prophets [pbuh] and Imams [as] are the manifestation of the Ultimate and Comprehensive Wisdom blessed to them by Allah [swt].

hudooth [the process of coming into being or existence] This term is used to refer to the existence of all the things in the world. The entire creation is described with this term. Only Allah [swt] is the exception who is eternally preexistent. Every existent needs a creator which is Allah [swt] to come into existence and so all the things are His creatures. Thus every existent has a beginning, a Creator, all its characteristics are acquired [and so *haadith*] and it has time of *fanaa*.

hulool [incarnation, permeation, penetration] The word indicates the transformation from one thing to other and to settle down in that particular object. God cannot incarnate into an object as that would mean His specific presence a particular space and time, which is impossible for God. Few people believe in the concept of the soul being transferred in some of the bodies. Few deviated sects believe in the penetration of Allah's soul in some gnostic scholar and few others like Hindus believe in incarnation where the soul transfers from one body to other in two different times.

inqadha [expiry, to be finished] This term refers to the nature of the creation that it has a date of expiry. The creation will not exist beyond that date. The whole creation is attributed to this characteristic.

qadeem [eternally pre-existent] This is one of the attributes of Allah [swt] referring to the concept of always present from infinity. Allah [swt] was, He is and He will always be. This term is used to indicate that He is not created; rather He is pre-existent. Unlike Him, His creatures are attributed to be *haadith*, the created ones. Thus all the gods beside Allah are not *qadeem* and were created.

zawaal [gradual destruction, weakening towards death, to perish etc] Everything in the world moves towards weakening, destruction and the death. The nature of the creation is formed in such a way that it has a time of expiry. This expiry time is *zawaal*. None of the creatures can be considered as a God because they are born or created for a limited time and undergo *zawaal* and thus these objects cannot be considered as gods. An example is the fact that every material object, living or non-living undergoes *zawaal* according to God's plan for it.

Index

Aas Ibn Wael Sahmi, 39
Abu Jahal, 39, 40, 57, 58, 60
Abudullah Ibn Umayyah, 39
Abul Bakhtari bin Hisham, 39
Adam, 23, 31, 35
angel, 21, 40, 41, 43, 46, 47
Atheism, 13, 37
Atheists, 3, 14, 24

bada, 66, 67, 68, 70
Bani Israel, 16, 57
batil, 65, 66
Bayt–ul–Muqaddas, 62, 63, 64, 65, 66
Bible, 22

Christians, 3, 6, 8, 9, 18, 19, 20, 22, 24

Dualism, 13, 37
Dualists, 3, 15, 27, 28, 29, 30

Egypt, 56
eternally pre-existent, 14, 19, 24, 25, 26, 27, 32, 72

fana, 33

haadith, 16, 19, 25, 26, 27, 32, 33, 71, 72
haq, 65, 66
hikmatal balighatal jamiah, 71
hudooth, 20, 24, 25, 26, 71
hulool, 32, 33, 72

Ibn Abi Umayyah, 40, 41, 42, 44, 45, 46, 51, 52, 53, 55, 56, 57
Ibrahim, 21, 58, 59, 60
Imam Ali, 13, 27, 36, 37
Imam Hassan Askari, 61, 65
Imam Zayn al-Abedin, 37
inqadha, 25, 72

Jerusalem, 62
Jews, 3, 6, 8, 9, 14, 15, 16, 17, 20, 22, 39, 61, 62, 63, 64, 65, 66, 67, 68, 70
Jibreel, 21, 63
Judaism, 5, 13, 37

Kaaba, 31, 35, 39, 62, 63, 64, 66, 67

Mecca, 31, 41, 48, 51, 55, 61
Medina, 7, 13, 41, 62
mehrab, 31
Messiah, 14, 19
Musa, 16, 17, 22, 57, 58

Noah, 23

Polytheism, 13, 37
Polytheists, 3, 30, 39
Prophet Ibrahim, 21
Prophet Isa, 14, 19, 20, 22, 23
Prophet Muhammad, 1, 3, 5, 7,
    9, 10, 11, 12, 13, 15, 18, 24, 27,
    28, 29, 37, 40, 62, 67
Prophet Musa, 16, 18, 57
Prophet Uzair, 14, 16
Prophethood, 52

qadeem, 14, 19, 24, 27, 32, 72
Qibla, 62, 63, 64, 65, 66, 67
Qur'an, 12, 41, 43, 48, 50, 58, 64
Quraysh, 39, 40, 60

Sanaviyas, 27, 28

Ta'ef, 41, 48, 52, 55
Torah, 16

Urwa bin Masu'd Thaqafi, 41

Walid Ibn Mughayra, 39, 41

zawaal, 33, 73

www.ingramcontent.com/pod-product-compliance
Lightning Source LLC
Chambersburg PA
CBHW071636040426
42452CB00009B/1653